HARVEY WANG'S
NEW YORK

FOREWORD BY

PETE HAMILL

PICTURES AND TEXT BY

HARVEY WANG

W.W. NORTON & COMPANY

NEW YORK & LONDON

W9-BZX-757

This book was sponsored by City Lore Inc.,
with a grant from The J.M. Kaplan Fund.
I am grateful to them for the support that
enabled me to finish the project.

·Introduction by Pete Hamill copyright © 1990 by Pete Hamill
Pictures and text by Harvey Wang copyright © 1990
by Harvey Wang

All rights reserved

Printed in Hong Kong by South China Printing Co. Ltd.
Typeset by Trufont Typographers
Designed by Katy Homans

First Edition

Library of Congress Cataloging in Publication Data

Wang, Harvey
Harvey Wang's New York / introduction by Pete Hamill.
p. cm.
ISBN 0-393-02914-X.—ISBN 0-393-30692-5 (pbk.)
1. New York (N.Y.)—Social life and customs—Pictorial works.
2. New York (N.Y.)—Occupations—Pictorial works.
3. New York (N.Y.)—Description—1981—Views. I. Title.
F128.37.W36   1990
974.7'1—dc20   90-44296
CIP

W.W. Norton & Company, Inc., 500 Fifth Avenue, New York, NY 10110
W.W. Norton & Company, Ltd., 30 Coptic Street, London WC1A 1PU

FOREWORD

There are at least three ways to look at the dense, layered, infuriating, and mysterious city of New York.

The first is with a sense of wonder, editing out reality, viewing the metropolis as some glorious steel-and-glass version of Oz. Alas, the romantic view is more and more difficult to conjure; it belongs to history or the imagination, not to the harder world of evidence.

The second is to gaze at the city as it is chronicled by New York's newspapers and television stations. You will almost certainly be appalled by the ferocity of *that* New York, the steady, grinding force of its poverty and violence, its vehement style, its penchant for melodrama, and its enthralled worship in the church of greed.

But there's another New York, if you have the eyes and the ears and the patience to recognize its existence. In these wonderful photographs, Harvey Wang takes us there and allows us to feel its existence. This is the New York of work and endurance. In this New York, human beings are driven by pride, not vanity. They have pride in craft and skill, in their abilities to do difficult tasks better than others. Most of them know what it means to master a difficult trade, and they have been content to practice that trade for a lifetime. How could we dispense with a Yiddish typesetter or the man who makes the Cyclone safe or the fellow who gives *platzes* in the Tenth Street Baths? Such men have understood what the greatest artists always know; the only true satisfaction comes from the *doing*, not the applause.

These photographs also suggest an older, tougher New York. In that New York, men and women lived their lives in the neighborhoods where they were born. They came out of the immigrant tradition, which placed family and work above all other values, and that mixture of family and work is the cement of the city. Their New York is seldom reflected in the newspapers or on the six o'clock news, because it is singularly devoid of melodrama. But only a fool would state that their lives do not contain the normal human portions of grief, triumph, complexity, and pain. Just look at the eyes of the people in these photographs. The eyes, and then the hands. The eyes allow entrance into the rugged terrain of their private lives; the hands suggest the way they have confronted the world: through work and mastery. These are not sprinters in the life of the city. They are not people who burned out young. They are not citizens ruled by fad and fashion. They don't perform their lives; they live them.

Such people never acquire enough honor. They don't often appear on the covers of magazines. They don't receive prizes. We pass them on the street without ever knowing them. But it is difficult to imagine a New York in which they did not practice their very special crafts. For that, and for his own obvious mastery of a difficult craft, I applaud Harvey Wang for bringing them at last up on the stage. If they seem oddly embarrassed by the sudden attention, the reason is simple: it's already time for them to go back to work.

PETE HAMILL
NEW YORK CITY 1990

ACKNOWLEDGMENTS

This book has been over four years in the making. In that time, so many people were generous with their help. I'd like to thank everyone who gave me ideas and references: Misha G. Avramowff (Project Ezra), John Belknap, Claire Bonner, Mary Boochever, Ruth Brown, Faye Chiang, Leon Cohen, Kathy Condon, *Crain's N.Y. Business*, Michael Daly, Meredith Davenport, Linda Dyett (*Great Shopping in Brooklyn*), Eddie Ellis, William Feehan, Howard Feigenbaum (Horn & Hardart), Marvin Frankel, Robert Glick, Pacey and Kenny Gomberg, Abby Gruen, Roberta Intrater, Eli Johnson, Deborah Karl, Alan Kaufman, Peter Kleinman, Charlie Liebman, Mary Lum, Ann McGettigan, David and Kate Morrison, Al Mottola, the *National Leader*, *New York Newsday*, the *New York Times*, Jack Newfield, Lt. Mike Puzziferri, Nina Rappaport, Peter Serling, *7 Days*, Roberta Singer, Eliza Smith, Herbert Steifel, Lissy Trachtenberg, the *Village Voice*, Lissa Ree Weinman, Steve Zeitlin, Robert Zimmerman. Sonja Williams-Wang, who saw me through to the end with love. My daughter Sakira, who occasionally allowed me to use the Macintosh. And, Sophia Mikaila Wang, born near deadline, whose smile calmed the frenzy. My family—Edna and Leo Wang and Fran and Skip Eichler—were supportive, as always. My "photo group" pals were always there to edit my choices down mercilessly: Donna Day, Pamela Duffy, Robert Maass, Randy Matasow, and Richard Sandler. I would never have finished this book if I didn't have the help of Beth Feehan, who kept me moving and organized, offered me ideas and support, and stepped in many times to save my life.

And most of all, without the faith and encouragement of Janet Byrne and my editor at Norton, James Mairs, this book would never have been made. I am forever grateful to them for making this happen, and for their friendship.

This book is dedicated to the New Yorkers it celebrates.

SIEGFRIED LIEBMAN

MANNEQUIN MAKER

For forty years, Siegfried "Charlie" Liebman made mannequins in a storefront workshop on Jerome Avenue in the Bronx. Charlie worked in his crowded shop from 1946 until his death in 1987. His career as a mannequin maker took off in 1942 when he originated the "egghead"—a simple shaped head used to display hats. One of Charlie's first customers, Lerner Shops, ordered about one hundred eggheads. Charlie always sold to downtown department stores, and in his later years his mannequins became fashionable in trendy Soho boutiques. Coming to the United States from Germany in 1938 to escape Nazi persecution, Charlie said, "Here I found freedom."

MICHAEL PELLICIONE

PHARMACIST

Michael Pellicione started working in his father's pharmacy when he was nine years old. Carmen Pellicione opened the tiny store on First Avenue at Twelfth Street in 1924 in what was then an Italian neighborhood. "I used to get out of school at 3:00 and I had to be in the store twenty minutes later to mop the floors and wash the showcases. I did that all through high school and college. When I got through with school, I had to come to work. I hardly got a day off," says Michael. "I went to Fordham College School of Pharmacy and liked it so much, I thought about becoming a doctor . . . but I had to work in the pharmacy. My father needed help." When the elder Pellicione died in 1963, Michael took over.

ISIDOR GLUCKSMAN

KOSHER BUTCHER

There used to be about twenty kosher butchers on this same Bronx block. Now there is just one left. "There are no more Jews here, just a few very old people," says Isidor Glucksman, who had his own shop for thirty-five years. But with the decline of the Jewish population, and the increase in rents, he closed up shop. Now he comes in two days a week for a few hours to work at Bob & Sam's Butcher Shop on Kingsbridge Road. "I mostly come in just to keep company," says Izzy. The other butchers in the shop tell the same story—their names too were once written in neon in storefront windows displaying pink chicken flesh and beef tongues. "The retail business here used to be ninety-nine percent in Jewish hands. There were delicatessens, bakeries, fish stores. Not anymore. This is the last."

13

JULIUS HANS

RABBINICAL TAILOR

Julius Hans specializes in making rabbinical garb out of elegant "kosher" materials. The overcoats, called *kapotes*, are made by hand out of silk or wool. Each coat takes about two and a half days to make. Julius came to New York in 1948 after surviving the Nazis in Poland by pretending to be a Catholic and living with the constant fear of being discovered. He went to church on Sundays, attended mass, and received communion. By the time he arrived in New York, he had forgotten how to speak Yiddish. His uncle Moishe, who had been in the custom-clothing business since the 1920s, took Julius in as an apprentice. In 1959, Moishe died, and Julius was going to close shop—but his customers wouldn't hear of it. He has made coats and pants for many of the famous Lubavitcher rabbis, including Rabbi Feinstein. Custom tailoring, Julius says, is a dying profession. "It's going out for ready-mades."

MARY MORISI

PASTA MAKER

The pasta at Morisi's Macaroni store on Fifth Avenue in Brooklyn is made on a Consolidated Macaroni Machine. The machine was manufactured in 1913, and was state-of-the-art for its day. The mechanical behemoth squeezes the flour and water mixture through brass dyes to form the various pasta shapes. Unlike modern commercial pasta, which is smooth and characterless, Morisi's pasta is rough-edged and thick. It takes twelve minutes to cook, and tastes like the pasta of turn-of-the-century Italian New York. At one time, every Italian neighborhood had its own macaroni shop. Mary Morisi and her husband, John, took over the Fifth Avenue macaroni shop in 1946. John made the pasta while Mary took care of customers and raised the family in the apartment upstairs. John died in 1981, but Morisi's is still a family affair, with son, Peter, and grandson, John-peter, making the pasta, and daughter, Savina, and granddaughter, Christine, helping customers out front. Mary makes the sauces, the lasagna, and the fillings for the ravioli and manicotti. In 1982 Peter started experimenting with new types of pasta. Morisi's now carries 225 varieties in 45 flavors, including favorites like asparagus ziti, beet capellini, peach cavetelli, calamari fettuccini, and goat cheese/walnut linguine.

JOHN CAUSARANO

BLACKSMITH

John Causarano, a blacksmith in Astoria, Queens, says that when he started work in the family business in 1921 there were "smithies" on every block. "My family has been shoeing horses for generations," he says. His shop, on Vernon Boulevard in Long Island City, was started by John's father, Dominick, who had come to the United States in 1905 from Mount St. Angelo, Italy. "We started when we were just kids, helping our dad. We used to have horses and wagons lined up and down the street and we could do thirty in a day," says Causarano, who works alongside his younger brother, Ralph. When Ralph retires, no family member will continue the business. The Causaranos stopped shoeing horses in 1952 as the few remaining horsedrawn vehicles were phased out. They now repair machine tools, hand tools and specialized tools for the construction trade and they repair and restore anything in steel.

19

EDDIE DAY

CYCLONE BRAKEMAN

Eddie Day has worked at the Cyclone, the lone remaining wood roller coaster in Coney Island, longer than any other employee. He began working at the Brooklyn institution in 1962 as chief brakeman. Before that, he worked on the Tornado, one of the many wood roller coasters in Coney Island that have been torn down. (The Bobsled, the LA Thompson, the Mile Skychasher, the Comet are all gone. The Thunderbolt remains, a decaying dinosaur.) The Cyclone was built in 1927. The nine cars that are used today are the original ones, and it's Eddie's job to keep them in working order. Eddie Day gets angry at the rumors of the Cyclone's closing: "Without the Cyclone, there is no Coney Island. Forget about Nathan's—that's for heartburn. . . ." Does Eddie ride the Cyclone? "I gave it up," he says.

ELLA BAKER

CIVIL RIGHTS ACTIVIST

Her name isn't as well known as Martin Luther King, Jr., or Stokely Carmichael, Jr., but to civil rights movement insiders, Ella Baker is a legendary figure. She moved to Harlem from the rural South in the late 1920s and started working with the Young Negroes Cooperative League, organizing food cooperatives in conjunction with the WPA. In the '30s she traveled throughout the South organizing for the NAACP, and in 1940 became their field secretary. In the '60s she was involved with the historic Montgomery bus boycott, and helped create the Southern Christian Leadership Conference and the Student Non-Violent Coordinating Committee (SNCC). Eleanor Holmes Norton, former chairwoman of the Equal Employment Opportunities Commission, said of Baker, "She has been at the cutting edge of initiating actions that led to great changes in this country." Ella Baker died in 1986. Paul Cowan wrote in the *Village Voice:* "Baker inspired many in the Southern Freedom movement with her patience and her ability to listen, not instruct. She embodied the best, the bravest, and the most humane part of the civil rights movement. The thousands of 'children' she left behind are a living legacy of her faith."

23

WILLIAM ITZKOWITZ

PILLOW MAKER

William Itzkowitz is holding court. "The small man is in trouble today. Between high rent and taxes, he doesn't have a chance." As he speaks he takes feathers from a large bag and pushes them into cotton ticking to make a pillow. The air around him is full of feathers, swirling around, landing everywhere. His 12-foot-by-30-foot shop on Ludlow Street is his fifth location. The business was started in 1922 by his father, a Hungarian Jew. The original store was more spacious and the rent more reasonable. Young Itzkowitz learned the trade by working. "Back then there was a demand. Now people run to the big stores and buy a piece of garbage. My pillows hold up for thirty to forty years. Feather and down is very expensive—it's murder." A standard pillow costs $22.00. Itzkowitz complains about finding good workers, the high cost of materials, the greed of landlords, the fussiness of customers, and concludes, "This is a hard business."

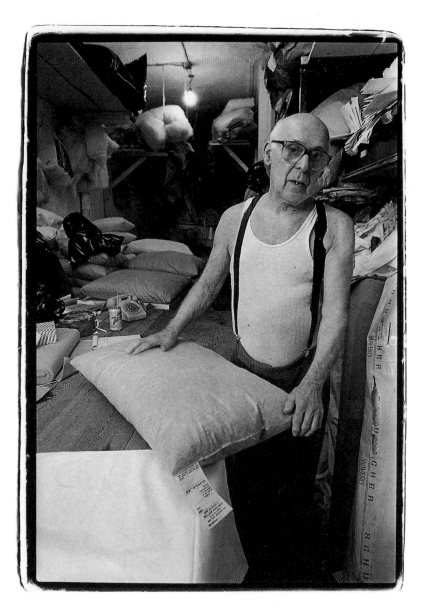

SIDNEY WEINER

TENTH STREET BATHS

Sidney Weiner spends his working hours naked in a 120-degree steam room. He works at the Tenth Street Russian Baths in the East Village giving washes and *platzes* to clients. (A *platza* is a brush made of dried oak leaves. Sidney will scrub a client with the leaves in the steam room. He must constantly pour ice-cold water on his face and body to endure the high temperature and thick steam.) The Tenth Street Baths is the last of its kind in New York City. There used to be dozens in Brooklyn, Manhattan, and the Bronx. The baths have a dry sauna, but most of the clients prefer the wet Russian steam room followed by a plunge in the icy cold pool. Upstairs, towel-clad men enjoy smoked fish, Russian specialties, juice, and beer, or they rest on cots. As a boy, Sidney used to go to Silver's, Staunch's, and the Washington Baths in Brooklyn with his father. Sidney has worked many jobs in his life. (Mostly he sold junk and bric-a-brac from a cart in Brooklyn.) He loves the baths—the kibitzing and schmoozing that happens when the old-timers get together. It helps him fill up his days. "What am I gonna do? Sit home and wait for death? Here, there are people."

27

SOL BERNHARDT AND
MOLLIE BALLIS

SOCIAL DANCERS, BRIGHTON BEACH

Eighty-three-year-old Sol Bernhardt and his 65-year-old dance partner, Mollie Ballis, dance exclusively with one another. They call
themselves "dance stylists" who through "a series of beautiful portraits bring out the showmanship of the dance." They do the rumba,
cha cha, merengue, waltz ("the dance of romance") and the tango
("the dance of love"). Sol says, "When Mollie and I dance we are very
eye-catching to watch." Though the partners have only been dancing together for fourteen years, Sol has been a social dancer for
sixty-five years. The partners got together in the summers at the
Brighton Beach Baths, which opened in 1910. The fifteen-acre beach
club borders Coney Island Avenue and the boardwalk and is a
Brooklyn institution. The baths' owners, Alexander Muss and Sons
of Miami, Florida, had been trying for many years to develop the
site into a luxury condominium complex despite community oppo-
sition. The owners decided to close the baths after the 1990 season
because of declining membership. In 1970, the baths had 13,000
members; by 1989 there were 2,200 members. Hy Cohen, manager
of the baths, said, "It simply is no longer commercially feasible for us
to keep it open."

DAVE HOFFMAN

NEWS VENDOR

Every afternoon rush hour Dave Hoffman stands poker-faced on the northeast corner of Forty-fifth and Lexington repeating, "Read all about it," in a classic news hawker's cry. He inherited the license to sell newspapers from his blind father, who began selling papers on Broadway over forty years ago. As a five-year-old boy, Hoffman would sit with his father in the tiny green booth watching customers toss change in a bowl. His father knew the sound of each denomination. Dave has occupied his Lexington Avenue booth for twenty-five years and is a fixture at the busy corner.

HELEN GIAMANCO

SALAD DEPARTMENT, HORN & HARDART

Horn & Hardart's first automat in Manhattan was opened in 1911 at Forty-sixth Street and Broadway. From the Depression to the 1950s Horn & Hardart was at its zenith of popularity. It offered good-quality food at cheap prices. People could sit for hours with a cup of coffee. Howard Feigenbaum, director of operations for the company, says that the invention of fast food as we know it today made the automat unable to compete because of the higher labor costs. Helen Giamanco works at the lone remaining automat on Forty-second Street and Third Avenue. She has worked for Horn & Hardart since 1946, longer than any other employee. Helen is head of the salad department, and moved from the automat at 545 Fifth Avenue to the Third Avenue location when it opened in 1957. The restaurant still does a decent business with a cafeteria, salad bar, and take-out food counter. Regulars come to the cafeteria for dishes Horn & Hardart has become famous for, including creamed spinach, baked beans, and macaroni and cheese. The antique German-made machines along the wall still dispense pies, sandwiches, and coffee.

33

PETE BENFAREMO

ITALIAN ICES MAKER

He's the King—the Lemon Ice King of Corona. His shop at the intersection of 108th Street and Corona Avenue is a summer mecca for sweaty New Yorkers. Pete's father bought the business in 1945, and Pete took over when he returned from World War II. Back then there were only two flavors—pineapple and lemon. "Every year I added one flavor," says Pete, "Now we have about thirty. We use fresh lemons, fresh oranges, fresh cherries. It's called Italian ices because it was made by Italians. Nowadays, it's just ices. Every flavor that I've made throughout my life, I've always made it as best as I can. If I make banana, it's gonna be banana. If I make pineapple, I put pineapple in." Pete and his wife of thirty-two years raised their two children above the store, and they still live there. The shop is open year-round and Pete says, "This business is seasonal. But it takes me three or four months in the winter to get straightened out, clean up, and fix the machines. By the time April rolls around I'm ready to open again." In the winter months, Pete has time to make jelly apples and reflect on his life. "A man is successful not by the money he makes. . . . It's what's around him that makes him happy. . . . I don't smoke, I don't drink. If I've got money in my pocket and a place to sleep, what more do I want?"

VICTOR GELLINEAU

SIGN PAINTER

As a kid growing up in New York in the 1920s, Victor Gellineau wanted to be a painter. One day, he saw a commercial artist and discovered a way to make some pocket money. He painted signs for his mother's grocer. More than fifty years later, Victor is still painting signs, but his canvas for the last seventeen years has been the office doors of the Empire State Building. Victor can be found on most days standing in front of a frosted glass door with a sable brush in his right hand resting on a maulstick. He does his lettering in a black-tinted glue called gold size. When the glue becomes tacky, he applies the gold leaf; when it's dry, he removes the excess to reveal the letters. Finally, he edges them in black with a #1 brush. The typeface he uses is Building Standard. The Empire State Building used to insist that all lettering be done in gold leaf, but in recent years they have allowed black letters for tenants who need to economize. Nowadays, many firms replace the old frosted glass doors with more modern styles. Victor's hand at 71 is still steady. He knows when to shorten an "L" or condense an "S" to arrive at a perfect fit. His edge line shows the varying thicknesses of handwork, but looks perfect to the untrained eye. About his work, he says, "It's tedious . . . you have to love it to do it. It's not a way to make a quick buck."

EDITTA SHERMAN

PHOTOGRAPHER

She is called "the Duchess of Carnegie Hall," and Editta Sherman has occupied her sun-drenched studio there since 1949. Walter Houston, Kirk Douglas, Sal Mineo, Elvis Presley, Henry Fonda, Somerset Maugham, Herman Wouk, and Shirley Booth have all had portraits made on her No. 7A Century Studio 8 × 10 camera. After living on farms in Maryland and Virginia, Editta and her husband moved to Martha's Vineyard, where she began her career as a photographer. Editta raised five children in her Carnegie Hall studio. She has an extensive collection of antique clothing, and was dubbed "the Duchess" because of a certain black dress and plume hat she sported on her outings. Or perhaps, Editta thinks, she received the nickname because "I've been growing old here."

EDWARD ROBB ELLIS

DIARIST

From the June 3, 1980, entry of Edward Robb Ellis's diary: "When I began writing my journal at the age of 16, I was unable to anticipate that it would expand into a huge chunk of Americana and ultimately be chosen as the greatest diary of the twentieth century. . . ." Now in its sixty-third year, Ellis's diary contains over 18 million words. The former newspaper reporter and author lives in a Chelsea apartment he shares with 15,000 books. Professor Gene Greesley, the custodian of the first sixty volumes of the Ellis diary at the University of Wyoming's American Heritage Center, calls Ellis "America's Pepys." Ellis writes about three pages a day and fills his pages with observations, details of everyday life, and philosophical musings. The English diary manufacturer Letts of London Ltd. has retained Ellis as a consultant, and he is designing a new line of diaries to be called the "Ellis Collection" for them. From Ellis's diary, July 22, 1980, after learning that the *Guinness Book of World Records* had decided to include his epic as the world's largest diary: "I have been forced to realize that my life was not lived in vain, that when I die I leave something of value, that my name may be known 200 years from now. . . . I have produced more words than those other great diarists—Pepys, Boswell, and Nin. Historians of the future may be grateful to me for leaving a record of life during this century."

AL GUIDO

GLAZIER

Al Guido often sits on the stoop of his Lower East Side glass shop watching the Chinese faces go by. There aren't many Italians left on Henry Street. It was different in 1932 when Al moved into the building, when Herbert Hoover was President. Al says, "There was a depression here. Very big." The glass shop's window cracked into pieces last year and a plywood board has replaced it. Spray painted on the plywood is "Manhattan Plate Glass Window." The glass in the store is mostly ancient and dusty, but Al can still find pieces to fit in the tenement windows, if he is asked to, and if his putty hasn't dried out. There hasn't been much business for Al, though. Mostly he drinks Seagram's and watches the world go by. To the north of Al's store is the Manhattan Bridge. Sometimes he looks at the bridge and wonders how many rivets were used to hold it together. "That bridge is across the river. They spin them cables like a spider. You know how a spider spins her web? They spin it from end to end. I didn't get much education, a little bit of junior high. But I'm not illiterate. I understand the basics of arithmetic, subtraction. . . . I want to learn diesel engines; I want to build a bridge. I want to know how the foundry works. How they melt the steel. . . . It runs like water. How do they roll a sheet of plate glass? They make it so perfect. How do they make them girders? I'd like to see those things."

REVEREND FLOYD KING

GOSPEL SINGER

"I preach in the churches and I preach on the radio. I was born in Camden, Alabama, 1909. I've been preaching for thirty-four years and I've been singing for sixty-eight years. And I love my job very, very much 'cause the Lord has been good to me. I've been singing with groups since I was seven years old. I sang with the Mack River Jubilee Singers. They are the oldest vocal group in the South. I've been in New York almost thirty years. . . . I am a member and the trainer of the five-man No Name Gospel Singers [of Crown Heights, Brooklyn]. . . . We travel a lot now. I teach *a cappella* singing. You have no music to hide behind so you have to do it right. No member of my group sits down. They call me trouble sometimes and they call me mean. I'm not trouble and I'm not mean; I just want to make sure they say it right and do it right. There's no instrument in the world can compete with you singing, if you train it. I was born with that gift. . . . I'm singing longer than the Dixie Humming Birds, longer than the Fairfield Four, longer than James Cleveland. . . ."

45

MONICA HICKEY

BRIDAL DIRECTOR

Beginning in 1900, the bridal shop at Henri Bendel's department store on Fifty-seventh Street was the destination for brides with an unlimited budget who desired one-of-a-kind dresses and personal attention, and who could afford to pay extravagant prices. In 1987, Bendel's closed the department. In the final days, the last Bendel's bride, Carolyn Frye, was fussed over by Bridal Director Monica Hickey and her staff of "consultants." The average cost of a Bendel's wedding dress was $2,500, but dresses costing $15,000 were not unheard of. "We're still doing the sort of things that we did fifty years ago," Miss Hickey said in 1987. "People love it. We're very friendly and nice. Our customers come from all over the country."

RICHARD BARNETT

BROOKLYN EQUESTRIAN

Richard Barnett of Boro Park began riding horses in Brooklyn in 1936. He recalls, "The stables then were like garages today. Around Prospect Park there used to be about seven stables." Dick says that a bridle path ran from Coney Island all the way to Prospect Park. "The park's bridle path was as good as you could find anywhere. It was watered and oiled regularly. It was four miles long, circled the park, cut by the zoo, went under a bridge, and went up to Grand Army Plaza. The way the park is laid out you know it was made with horses in mind." The Culmitt on Caton Place is the last remaining stable around Prospect Park. "Things have changed considerably. Out in Jersey and on Long Island horses are still a big thing. In Brooklyn it just dissipated—I guess on account of the lack of places to ride and the rising property values. Across the street was a place called Teevans. It was the most exclusive riding stable. They had the best music ride where folks would come in full dress and listen to live music. People came from all over up until the forties. Now it's a bowling alley."

JOE BAFFI

BOXING TRAINER

The afternoon sun reflects off the barren industrial buildings of downtown Brooklyn into Gleason's Gym on Front Street. Inside, the odor of sweat fills the large room. In practice rings, young men in gloves and bandages circle, dance, and throw punches at each other. In one ring, a skinny 17-year-old watches as 71-year-old Joe Baffi demonstrates a defensive posture. In his youth, Joe was an amateur fighter in his Brooklyn neighborhood. He lost in his first outing and spent his working years as a welder, longshoreman, and postal worker. Now he trains youngsters how to box. Joe has worked at all the old gyms—Stillmans, the Solar Gym, the Pioneer Gym, and the old Gleason's on Thirtieth Street. They're all gone. "I don't do it for the money. I take kids away from the street, away from drugs, the bad life. I watch their legs, their eyes. I'd rather they do their fighting in the gym, not on the streets. I have a 17-year-old. He can't fight. I might be dead before he can fight. But I still have a dream to fulfill . . . to have a champ," he says.

MAX FUCHS

USED-CLOTHING DEALER

Nestled between Wah Yu, a magazine store, and New Sam Kee, a fruit and vegetable vendor, is Nathin and Max Clothing. The proprietor, Max Fuchs, has been in this location since 1928. The business is the only non-Chinese one on the block, but when he opened, "The neighborhood was all Italian, and a big used-clothing market. It was all clothing stores on the street, all along Bayard Street and Elizabeth Street and a few on the Bowery. On Elizabeth Street, you could rent a bin for three dollars and sell your old clothes. The elevated train was on the Bowery until the '40s," Max recalls. Max's partner of forty-five years, Louis Nathin, died in 1974. They started in a smaller space in 1927 at 61 Bayard Street. He sells mostly new clothes and continues to sell uniforms to the court officers who work nearby in Foley Square. "We used to sell more uniforms—policemen, firemen, letter carriers, conductors, motormen, doormen, bellhops," he says. During prohibition, Max rented the back room to a speakeasy. The interior of the store hasn't changed. Max tells a visitor: "The store is the same now as it was in 1928. The floor is the same; the tin ceiling is the same—everything is the same. Only you are here today."

LOUIS LUBRANO

LONGSHOREMAN

Until the city of Philadelphia got into the act twenty-two years ago, the Port of New York handled a lot more cocoa beans. Douglas Martucci, of Continental Terminals in Brooklyn, says that there were probably ships unloading once a week. Nowadays, ships bearing cocoa beans from places like Africa and South America arrive in New York about six times a year. Cocoa is the only crop that cannot be containerized, because the beans give off heat, creating a terrarium effect in the containers, which ruins the beans. It is called a "break-bulk" crop. Before containerization and the development of the container pier at Port Newark, Brooklyn's break-bulk piers stretched from the Army Terminal at Fifty-ninth Street to Front Street. Continental Terminals is a public warehouse where green coffee beans and raw cocoa beans are stored after being off-loaded, until the importers sell them to the roasters or manufacturers. Longshoreman Louis Lubrano has been unloading ships since 1952. He has "B" seniority on a scale of A to I. Though in his 50s, Lubrano still manages to work five days a week. He was part of a crew of one hundred longshoremen supplied by Universal Stevedore Company to unload 63,000 bags of Ivory Coast cocoa from a Czech ship. When he began his waterfront career, he earned $2.60 an hour. Now his hourly wage is $18.00.

DOMINIC BENCIVENGA

ROPE FENDER MAKER

From the 1700s and probably earlier, small ships used rope fenders to protect their hulls. But by the late 1970s, discarded rubber tires had replaced rope as the material of choice for fenders. Dominic Bencivenga, an employee of Turecamo Coastal and Harbor Towing Corporation since 1948, used to make rope fenders for his company's fleet of tugboats. Each tugboat needed four or five fenders, including the important bow fender. Dominic explains the process: "We'd start with a strap of approximately ten feet, and build it out till it had a round look in the center. We'd take a piece of seven-inch line, fold it in half, splice the center of it, and on each end put a thimble. So now you'd have a strap with a thimble on each end. Then we'd come in on the ends about six inches from each thimble and put a coarse of line the length of that strap. Each layer was decreased by six inches more, so that the thickest part of the fender was right at the center of the bow. After that was done, we'd put the knitting on it, which holds the fender together, and then we'd put the whiskers on, which were short pieces of rope, woven in to protect the knitting." It would take two men three to four days to do one bow fender, some of which weighed over a thousand pounds, and lasted more than two years. Since rubber replaced rope, Dominic has not had much occasion to practice this craft, but he did recently make a rope fender for the South Street Seaport Museum, to be used on a reproduction 1850s New York Pilot Gig.

HERMAN BUCKWALD

FISH DEALER, FULTON FISH MARKET

Since 1924 Herman Buckwald has been going to work at the Fulton Fish Market when most New Yorkers are just going to sleep. By one in the morning, he is on the phone in his tiny office at C. G. Wadman & Company, buying fish from Maine to Florida. "If it swims in salt water, I sell it," Herman says. Surviving the nocturnal world of the fish market requires many skills. "This is a rough business," says the 84-year-old fish dealer. "There is a tough element in the market. Used to be a lot of ex-cons down here. But they've mostly disappeared . . . either they're floating in the East River or they've died." According to Herman, the market today is the same size that it was when he started, but the demand for fish has decreased. "The old generation ate fish, but today, they don't go for it too much. Today they mostly eat seafood—shrimp, crabs, lobster. Take eels. Every year at Christmas the demand for eels has decreased because the old timers who do go for eels die. The same with gefilte fish . . . eventually the same thing will happen." The market opens at 3 A.M. on Mondays, and 4 A.M. the rest of the week. Herman works until about noon, goes home, has a snack, and then sleeps for three or four hours. He wakes up around dinner time to make business calls, then goes back to sleep until 11 P.M. The Fulton Fish Market was already well established on the East River when the Brooklyn Bridge was built over one hundred years ago. Until about fifteen years ago, the fish mostly arrived by ship, but now in the predawn hours it is flown and trucked in from all over the world. Wholesalers, retailers, hotel and restaurant suppliers move among the iced crates, fillet tables, massive swordfishes lying on the pavement, and hand trucks to make their deals.

MARTHA GRONSKI

POLAR BEAR CLUB

In Russia, they are called The Walrus Club, in Denmark, The Freezers, but in Coney Island and many other parts of the world they are known as The Polar Bears. What they all have in common is a belief in the therapeutic value of winter ocean swimming. The Coney Island club is one of the largest around, with fifty winter swim members and about 150 auxiliary members who support the club but do not indulge in winter swims. Founded in 1903 by Bernarr Macfadden, the club was patterned after its European counterparts. Martha Gronski became the first female member of the Coney Island Polar Bear Club when she joined in 1964. Originally from Sweden, Martha has lived in New York since 1929. She hasn't taken a winter swim since 1988, but she does join the club at their weekly gatherings on the boardwalk at Stillman Avenue in Coney Island on Sundays at noon.

PETE PETERKIN

AUTO MECHANIC

"First car I ever 'timed' was a 1922 Buick. It had wooden spoke wheels—boy, that was an old one. I was a born mechanic. I just picked it up. In 1941, when I went to the service, they sent me to mechanic's school in Virginia. That's when I got the book learning." The speaker is Doam "Pete" Peterkin. He is retired but early each morning he comes to Owls Head Service in Bay Ridge, Brooklyn, to open shop and help out. Pete was born in South Carolina, and after the war he came to New York to stay. "It was real rare to be a black mechanic. I got a job, but the owner took me out of the garage to pump gas." Pete says, "There's nothing new. It's all been done before. Today's mechanics have it easy. We had to make our own tools. We didn't have a computer to find problems. Back then nobody told you nothing." Reflecting on how his color kept him from fixing engines, he says, "Blacks today have quite an opportunity. They can work on any car."

SOLOMON SALZBURG

Up until the early 1950s the area east of First Avenue between Houston Street and Fourteenth Street was a bustling center of Jewish life. Puerto Rican immigration to New York City in the 1950s started to change the area that is now called "Loisaida"—the Latino residents' name for the Lower East Side. Solomon Salzburg lives on the corner of Fourth Street and Avenue C and is a remnant of the Jewish life that once dominated the area. Born in 1902 in Galicia ("When Franz Joseph was emperor"), Solomon came to the United States in 1920 with an uncle. His first residence in New York City was on St. Marks Place. His uncle got him a job as a busboy in the Catskills, where many Jews summered. "I made $300 for the season. I felt like the richest man in America, after Rockefeller," recalls Sol. After the summer, Sol found work as a waiter, but he was laid off in 1929 when cafeterias became popular. Before then, "There was no such thing as self-service. Cafeterias introduced that. . . . The waiters picketed," says Sol. He didn't get a job again until the late 1930s when the country mobilized for war. The rest of Sol's working days were spent in restaurants and in hair salons where he cut ladies' hair. He has lived in Loisaida for most of his life. Sol was moved to a low-rent, city-owned tenement when his building burned down. Every morning, he leaves his apartment and walks past the boarded-up and converted synagogues on his way to Tompkins Square Park, where he passes his days.

JOEY FAYE

BURLESQUE COMEDIAN

At 80 years of age, Joey Faye is still called upon to act in burlesque show revivals. He has spent his life on various stages, and is credited with bringing a new type of comedy into burlesque. "Before me, the comics used dialect and wore baggy pants and putty noses. I was the well-dressed comic with loud clothes and a little comedy hat," he says. Joey was born in Manhattan in 1909 and now lives in Staten Island. He got into show business by performing at the Amateur Nights sponsored by movie houses during the Depression. "I found I could get a guaranteed two dollars every night, win or lose," Joey recalls. "I made my New York debut at Minsky's Burlesque in the Republic Theater in 1931 and I remained with him until 1938. Burlesque was the poor man's entertainment. In burlesque a line of girls come out dancing and singing, then they leave. Then two comics come out, usually with a girl, and do a scene. Then out comes the first strip. Then the chorus girls come out and do a number. Then, depending on how good the show is, there's a series of four or five strips." After the days of burlesque, Joey worked as a comedian in bars and hotels in New York City, Chicago, and the Catskills. "I'm best known for being a fruit in the Fruit of the Loom commercials, but I've also done thirty-one Broadway shows including *The Man Who Came to Dinner* and *Waiting for Godot*. About twenty years ago I did two hundred fifteen-minute films called *Mack and Meyer for Hire* with Micky Deans. They were shown on local television. The films weren't as good as Laurel and Hardy but not as bad as the Three Stooges. We had a hell of an audience. All the great burlesque houses are long gone; they're mostly porno theaters now."

SAUL FROMKIN

WOODWIND REPAIRMAN, TIMES SQUARE

On the walls of Saul Fromkin's instrument repair shop on Forty-sixth Street were photographs of some of the world's greatest sax players. Many of them were inscribed. From Kit McClure: "Thank you for keeping my act together." From Bud Freeman: "To the best in his field." From Sonny Rollins: "For Saul—the musician's friend." From Junior Cook: "To Saul—a true artist." Top jazz artists brought their horns to Saul to have them "oversauled" and "Fromkinized." One photo had a telling caption: "Saul, I'll just wait here till you fix my horn (as usual). One day I'll pay you too." Saul went into business for himself in 1955. He did well his first year, mostly repairing school instruments. He soon began to specialize in wood-winds for professional musicians. He says, "I was just enamored of these great players. I couldn't play anymore [after an auto accident] and I felt if I could do a good job, I'd be transferring myself through their playing." Saul's shop soon became a meeting place for the saxophone legends and trendsetters of the day. "In my shop there was always a place to sit. Guys knew they could come and crash. They'd come into town with no money, and no place to stay. Sometimes they'd be drunk, and I'd let them spend the night, sleep it off." In 1989 Saul's landlord raised the rent 700 percent, forcing him to close shop. He moved to Florida to repair school instruments again. He lamented, "The little craftsmen are all disappearing. Tens of thousands of small businesses have left New York in the past few years. Around Times Square, everyone is panicking because all the support businesses are closing."

GEORGE WILLIAMS

SELTZER BOTTLER

"I go to sleep dreaming of seltzer bottles," says George Williams, who estimates he fills 3,000 empty glass canisters with a mixture of filtered water and carbon dioxide gas every day. He works at G & K Beer Distributors in Canarsie, Brooklyn. Kenny Gomberg, grandson of G & K founder Moe Gomberg, says that at the beginning seltzer was the biggest part of the business. Now it's a novelty. George started in the business about thirty-five years ago at Cohen Seltzer Works in Boro Park, one of the dozens of bottlers in business back then. There are just a few left that fill the antique Czech-made bottles with a Barnett and Foster Syphon (*sic*) Filler machine that dates back to 1910. Says George, "The younger generation mostly goes for flavored sodas."

71

JACK BETTEIL

TELEVISION REPAIRMAN

"I've been in this particular location for thirty-seven years. Unfortunately my lease is up and my landlord wants to double my rent, plus seven hundred fifty dollars a year real estate tax. So I'm closing up. This is a neighborhood business, a one-man shop. I do everything myself," says Jack Betteil of Speed TV in Flushing, Queens. He repairs television sets, VCRs, and hi-fis out of his dusty storefront workshop. "When I started, it was mostly tube radios. In the sixties, televisions surpassed radios. These days, you can buy a radio for twenty-five bucks. People throw them out." Born in Poland, Jack survived the Holocaust and immigrated to the United States in 1947. He is an easy-going man who knows his neighbors and waves at them as they pass by his store. He is flexible with his charges, forgoing payment for elderly and impoverished clients. "People like me are fading away," he says.

PASQUALE SPENSIERI

GRINDER

Pasquale Spensieri's 1955 Dodge truck has logged 108,000 miles on Brooklyn streets searching for dull knives, scissors, and lawn mowers to sharpen. His father, uncle, and cousins were also grinders who worked out of trucks. The family traces its origins to the Campo Basso region in Italy, which is famous for its grinders. Pasquale's route takes him to different neighborhoods on different days. He works Kings Highway, Canarsie, Avenue V, Nostrand Avenue, Flatbush Avenue, Fifth Avenue, and Bay Ridge visiting restaurants, upholstery shops, and pizza places along the way. When he started thirty-six years ago he charged 50 cents per blade. Now he gets $2.00.

KAY DEMITRIOU

BARBER

Kay Demitriou has been a fixture on upper Broadway since the 1940s. He has cut generations of heads, has people coming to him from all over the world, and commands such loyalty that by his estimate, a third of his customers come to his shop from New Jersey. He says the shop he owns on 104th Street and Broadway is the oldest barber shop in New York City. Built by an Italian immigrant in 1907, the shop has the original chairs, mirrors, hot-towel steamer, tin ceilings, and tile floors. The Carrara marble was imported from Italy. Looking around the barbershop, one can imagine the days when six barbers, two manicurists, and a shoeshine man were kept busy here. Now it is only Kay, who can do a flattop in three minutes, but prefers to take his time. "I don't rush myself. My customers are happy, they sit and wait. I don't rush anyone out," he says. The London-born barber began cutting hair at ten years of age. He can do any style from the '40s to the '90s, and has been called upon to cut for Broadway shows. He says he invented a cut called the Semi Madison Avenue which is a longer version of the standard conservative short cut. Kay says he was the one who introduced long hair. "I encouraged it. The *New York Times* wrote about me in 1964. I have the clipping in the shop."

ROBERT L. HARLEY

THE OLD PRINT SHOP

When Robert L. Harley got his first job with The Old Print Shop in 1929 after graduating from New York University the previous year, he never thought it would also be his only job. He walks the seven blocks to work five days a week and says, "I like almost everything in the store." The Old Print Shop has been in business since 1898. The shop sells mostly lithographic and etched prints, and nineteenth- and twentieth-century modern master prints. Though its lower Lexington Avenue location is off the beaten track for art buyers, The Old Print Shop's vast selection attracts knowledgeable customers. Harley started working for the current owner's father as a jack of all trades. He has swept floors and has sold art to presidents and governors.

ASTON ROBINSON

WAITER, GAGE & TOLLNER

To step into Gage & Tollner from the busy Fulton Street Mall in Brooklyn is to step back in time. On the mall, the garish storefronts of fast-food restaurants like Bojangles and Roy Rogers compete with the screaming signs of electronics stores and the flashing lights of discount-clothing outlets. In the restaurant gas lamps illuminate the 120-year-old landmark interior, which resembles a Pullman dining car. (The Gage & Tollner interior is the only one in a New York City restaurant to be declared a landmark.) Until the mid 1970s only black waiters worked in the restaurant. Years ago, customers would have favorite waiters, and every waiter had his own customers. The old timers are all retired but some of them had worked for over sixty years. Waiter Aston "Robby" Robinson has been at Gage & Tollner for seventeen years. He has weathered the years when the restaurant's reputation declined. In 1987, new owner Peter Aschkenasy hired the famous southern chef Edna Lewis and they have worked to restore Gage & Tollner to its former glory.

81

BILL NEWMAN

BOWLING ALLEY MECHANIC

Bill Newman has been working in bowling alleys since he was 18. His first job was giving out shoes at the Imperial Lanes in Woodside. He was a pin chaser for a while before he learned to be a mechanic. In the early 1960s, Bill recalls, bowling was at its peak. Many of the places Bill has worked—Roosevelt Bowl-a-Rama, Astoria Lanes, and the Imperial Lanes—have closed, victims of dwindling clientele and high rents. He is currently night mechanic at 34th Avenue Bowl in Woodside, a busy thirty-five lane alley that opened in 1959. It is one of a handful still in business in Queens.

BENESH HOROWITZ

TYPESETTER

The Yiddish-language newspaper the *Daily Forward* started printing in 1897. At its peak in the 1930s, 250,000 copies were sold daily to Jewish immigrants from Eastern Europe, and forty-two men worked in the composing room. Now the *Forward* is a weekly with 25,000 readers and five full-time employees who set articles into type in the basement composing room of their Thirty-third Street offices. They use the Mergenthaler Linotype machine—a mammoth 80-year old relic. Each line of letters is formed in hot lead, and each headline is hand set. Once, all newspapers were set in "hot type." Now the *Forward* is one of the last ones in New York using the Linotype machine. Benesh Horowitz is the foreman of the composing room. Before coming to the *Forward*, he worked for twenty years at the *Day Journal*, a Yiddish paper that folded in 1972.

SOL COHEN

FOUNDER, EASTERN SEWING MACHINE

Twenty years ago, every store on Twenty-fifth Street between Broadway and Seventh Avenue was involved in the sewing-machine business. Twenty-fifth Street and the surrounding blocks were the world's marketplace for industrial sewing machines; people came from all over to buy, sell, and exchange them. Many of the small shops were run by mechanics who had gone out on their own. Most of them have closed up, because they were dependent on the New York needle trades. As the shoe, handbag, and garment manufacturers succumbed to imports and rising rents, the supporting industries went with them. One of the few old-timers left is Sol Cohen of Eastern Sewing Machine, who started his company after World War II. Sol's son, Leon, who joined him in 1958, says, "Our business is not dependent on New York, but it's mostly out of town and foreign. In the used-machine business, quite a bit is export. We sell to the Orient, Central and South America and occasionally to Europe."

HENRY SAHAGIAN

PHOTO-ENGRAVER

Before offset lithography took over, there were fifty-two photo-engraving shops in New York City that served the letterpress printing industry. The photo-engravers converted photographs and newspaper and magazine pages into copper printing plates. But like letterpress printing, photo-engraving is a disappearing trade. There are only two union shops left in New York. Henry Sahagian followed his brother into the business in 1946. (Brother Frank started in 1937 at Pictorial—his uncle's firm.) Henry spent eight years as a messenger boy for Pictorial before he became an apprentice. The apprenticeship period lasted six more years before he was qualified to be a photo-engraver. Henry left Pictorial to work for Mercury when his brother took over that failing company. "We formed a co-op with ten partners to keep it in existence. . . . We were all close friends and I tried to keep the boys working," says Frank.

NAFTALIE LICHTENSTEIN

MAZHGIEKH, MATZOH BAKERY

From January until April the Pupa & Zehlem Matzoh Bakery in Williamsburg, Brooklyn, is a hub of activity. The bakery's one product—*shmurah* matzoh—is essential for Orthodox Jews observing the eight-day holiday of Passover. *Shmurah* means watched or supervised, and every step of the process, from the cutting of the wheat and the grinding of the flour to the baking of the dough in a coal- and wood-fired oven, is carried out under the watchful eye of 70-year-old Roumanian-born Naftalie Lichtenstein, the *mazhgiekh* (kosher supervisor). The bakery has been producing matzoh for the Orthodox Pupa and Zehlem congregations in Williamsburg for thirty-five years, and the members of the congregations supply all the labor for the production of the unleavened bread.

MAX MORRISON

SCRAP METAL COLLECTOR

Max Morrison is always on the lookout for other people's discarded trash. Not all trash—only metal. "Anything that's metal is salable. Aluminum, copper, brass bring in the most money," says the 97-year-old grandfather of seven. "I avoid iron because it's too heavy." Max's only concession to age is that he needs one of the grandkids to drive him and his booty to Irving's Scrap Metal on Ditmas Avenue in Brooklyn, where it is sorted, weighed, and exchanged for cash. "I retired ten years ago. After I gave up working, I needed something to do. I would pick up old television sets, not because I needed it, but just to keep busy. I can't sit still on a chair reading comics or walk around the streets doing nothing. I certainly do enjoy collecting metal. It's legitimate, not too heavy. I just do it so I can have something to do, and I get money for it," he says. Max spent his life repairing, building, and selling electronics. He built radios before they were commercially available. In the 1930s he had a repair shop on Franklin Street near Union Street in Brooklyn.

ADAM PURPLE (REV. LES EGO)

URBAN GARDENER

By the early 1970s, much of Manhattan's Lower East Side had become a desolate, abandoned place where prostitutes and junkies flourished. In the midst of this, Adam Purple started a garden in the backyard of his tenement building on Eldridge Street. In time, the surrounding tenements were torn down and Purple's circular *Garden of Eden* grew to 1,500 square feet and included forty-five fruit and nut trees. He carted off tons of refuse and created virgin topsoil with horse manure from Central Park as well as his own "night soil." He used simple tools and raw muscle power. Adam envisioned the garden expanding until it replaced the asphalt and skyscrapers of New York. The city had other ideas and, after a protracted battle, the garden was bulldozed in 1986 to make way for a federally funded housing project.

RICHARD THOMPSON

CUSTOMER, MERKEN'S LUNCHEONETTE

Merken's Luncheonette on Myrtle Avenue in Ridgewood, Queens, is an old-fashioned place where ice cream is made daily in a thirty-five-year-old machine. The store opened in 1921, and the name changed in 1953 when Henry Merken purchased it. They made candies, chocolate syrup, and whipped cream. Richard Thompson, a long-time Ridgewood resident who retired in 1986 from Hall Street Cold Storage, stops in every day for a sundae.

LEE WONG

RESTAURANT OWNER

The name of the restaurant, "New Toyson," is displayed on the neon sign out front in mock Chinese letters. Surrounding the name is "Chop Suey" and "Chow Mein." Lee Wong ("all my friends call me Leo") opened the restaurant in 1951, when Cantonese food was the only kind of Chinese cuisine you could find in the United States. His business is family run. One granddaughter who helps out jokes that the only way to get out of the restaurant is to get married. Leo's family history is typical of many Chinese in the United States. His grandfather came in the late 1800s to work in a laundry in Massachusetts (the only work available to Chinese once the railroads were finished). Nowadays, the New Toyson is rarely busy. But at 85 years of age, Lee plans to keep the restaurant open. "My business is like my baby. . . . It's something I nursed, and I'd hate to give it up. I don't need the money, but I built this place—I'd like to see it keep going."

LEON DYCZKO

STOREFRONT INSURANCE

The plate-glass window on Ninth Street says, "Lawyer, Real Estate, Notary, Insurance." Inside is an old-time office, with crowded files and well-worn furniture. John Dyczko sits at a rear desk puffing on his trademark cigar, sorting through insurance claims. His older brother, Leon, is counting dollar bills given to him by an elderly Polish woman who visits every month to pay her rent. The brothers manage eleven buildings in the East Village for absentee landlords. Their office is also the place where longtime residents of the East Village can pick up and exchange gossip on neighborhood goings-on. The storefront office was begun in 1946 by Leon's now-deceased older brother, Joseph, and his godfather, a real estate man.

VERONICA PARKER JOHNS

OWNER, SEASHELLS UNLIMITED

Veronica Johns's store, Seashells Unlimited, on Third Avenue in Manhattan, specialized in mollusk shells. She also carried coral and starfish, but the bulk of her stock came from among the 100,000 species of mollusks that inhabit the earth's oceans. "My interest in shells is primarily beauty," the former mystery-book writer says. The dark store was a magical place, where beauty could be found in glass cases, metal drawers, and overflowing cardboard boxes. Miss Johns bought the business in 1963 and the store closed in 1988.

CARMINE VENEZIA

BAND LEADER

Two hundred and fifty times a year, Carmine Venezia and his marching band play their sad hymns at Chinese funerals on Bayard Street in Chinatown. Though the 87-year-old trombone player has been doing funerals for only about fifteen years, he has worked steadily as a musician since 1928. "Before the funerals, I was the leader in the Italian feast for twenty-five years. It's been my profession, my bread and butter. I raised four children. I played dance halls, theaters. I was with RKO for seven years. I played all phases of music, from jazz to Dixieland. I've played with Jewish bands, German bands, Irish bands. You name it, I've played it," the band leader says. Carmine's band is a sight to behold—about twelve musicians, none of them Chinese, in somber overcoats marching in front of the hearse as it proceeds down Bayard Street. Surrounding them are tear-drenched Chinese faces. Having a funeral band is not a Chinese custom. According to Carmine, the Italians who used to live in the area had big bands at their funerals, and the new residents just adopted it. Though Carmine is approaching 90, he says, "With my trombone in my hands I feel ten years younger." Making people happy with his music has always given him satisfaction. "Once a priest told me, 'Without you, this funeral would have been a dud.'"

TOM RELLA

GRAVEDIGGER

Tom Rella is a gravedigger at one of the few cemeteries where graves are still dug by hand. The Jewish Bayside Cemetery in Ozone Park is over one hundred years old and the plots are so close together that it is impossible to get a backhoe in to dig the graves. Tom Rella has been working at Bayside for six years. He enjoys the work— "Nobody is on your back." The worst part of the job for Tom is the disinterments. He says it's the strangest thing he's ever done. "You go into the grave with a little rake and collect all the bones. You have to get the head—that's the important thing. . . . At first I'd get dizzy and sick during a disinterment, but once you get over the odor, it's not too bad."

AFTERWORD

I started taking photographs for this book when the Ninth Street Bakery in the East Village closed for a weekend and remained shut for about five months. The bakery is a small, disorganized place where devotees buy nine-grain bread and corn muffins out of cardboard boxes. Harry Wolk's illness was responsible for the bakery's closing for those five months, and when Harry recovered the bakery reopened. But New York

City almost lost another institution. Harry's parents started selling baked goods in 1928, specializing in day-old bread. By 1938 they had three locations which were all located near push-cart markets. The closing of the Ninth Street Bakery would not have shaken the city, but as places like Harry's disappear, so goes an intimate, humanizing part of New York. In recent years, all over town, small businesses have been closing. Sometimes, the proprietors retire.

Often areas get "redeveloped" (Times Square) or "gentrified" (East Village) and rents skyrocket beyond the means of the small shop-keeper. And neighborhoods change. One immigrant group gives way to another, and slowly shops catering to the older group lose their clientele.

I've always had an interest in these pockets of "holdout" New York. As a high-school student I befriended Mrs. Sullivan, who sat in a tiny green booth on Fortieth Street and Seventh Avenue selling newspapers. Seventy-four years old, Mrs. Sullivan supported her paralyzed 85-year-old husband in a run-down Times Square hotel. She was deaf, and nearly blind, and called everyone

"Pop." In her high, cackling voice she'd tell stories of her youth in 1930s New York as a "gay pleasure girl." In Bay Ridge, Brooklyn, all that is left of a once-vibrant Norwegian community is The Atlantic restaurant. The fifty photographs in the book are but

a fraction of those I shot. There was Natalie Spatz at Rat-

ner's Dairy Restaurant on Delancey Street (where my grandfather made a meal out of a cup of soup and a basket of rolls). Dana O'Connell, the Ziegfeld Girl, Saul Dunkelblau at Butterfield Market—an old-time full-service grocery store on Lexington Avenue. Nettie Zimmerman, who was the notary pub-

lic at the Ansonia Hotel on upper Broadway. Gonzalo Placsenci, a pool-hall owner in Sunset Park, Brooklyn. Sol Gever, one of the last shoe manufacturers left in the city, who said: "Everything is going. . . . all the small industries—handbags, shoes—all because of the imports. I feel like the last of a kind. Maybe I should retire . . . but nobody wants to buy a shoe factory." Herbert Steifel, the "Zipper King," Mar-

tin Goldstein of Paradise Pawnbrokers in the Bronx, and the sail maker Herbert Hild, who has been in the business for forty-three years on City Island and said to me: "The old skills and trades that we knew of years ago are almost

extinct right now. In fact, we're probably one of the last sail makers in

the country who still are able to perform the old ways of handwork."

Subjects for the book were found in various ways. Word of mouth, newspaper clippings, recommendations from friends. Sometimes I sought out a specific subject. Many times, I was too